THE GOLDEN YEARS OF RAILROADING

SANTA FE IN THE MOUNTAINS

Three passes of the West: Raton, Cajon, and Tehachapi

GEORGE H. DRURY

KALMBACH BOOKS

Printed in the United States of America

Book Design: Sabine Beaupré
Cover Design: Kristi Ludwig
Copy Editor: Mary Algozin

On the cover: Tripleheaders weren't uncommon on Raton Pass. The second section of train 20, the *Chief*, all mail and express, starts out of Raton with 2-10-2s 3872 and 934 assisting the 4-8-2 road engine, No. 3718. The lead 2-10-2 carries its Elesco feedwater heater down on the pilot (only a few Santa Fe engines had them in the usual location atop the smokebox) for ease of washing out the device, necessary in bad-water territory. Photo by R. H. Kindig, March 28, 1946.

Publisher's Cataloging in Publication
(Prepared by Quality Books Inc.)
Drury, George H.
    Santa Fe in the mountains : three passes of the west — Raton, Cajon, and Tehachapi / George H. Drury. — Waukesha, WI : Kalmbach Pub., 1995.
    p. cm. — (Golden years of railroading ; 1)
    Includes bibliographical references and index.
    ISBN 0-89024-229-1

    1. Railroads—United States—History—Pictorial works. 2. Raton Pass (Colo. and N.M.)—Pictorial works. 3. Cajon Pass (Calif.)—Pictorial works. 4. Tehachapi Pass (Calif.)—Pictorial works. 5. Atchison, Topeka, and Santa Fe Railway Company—History. I. Title.

TF20.D78 1995   625.1'009'73
                                 QBI95-20345

CONTENTS

Tripleheaders weren't uncommon on Raton Pass. The second section of train 20, the *Chief*, all mail and express, starts out of Raton with 2-10-2s 3872 and 934 assisting the 4-8-2 road engine, No. 3718. The lead 2-10-2 carries its Elesco feedwater heater down on the pilot (only a few Santa Fe engines had them in the usual location atop the smokebox) for ease of washing out the device, necessary in bad-water territory.
Photo by R. H. Kindig, March 28, 1946.

ATCHISON, TOPEKA & SANTA FE RAILWAY

The Santa Fe is North America's best known railroad, the result of those red-and-silver diesels, a historic route, a wild-west setting, and decades of appearances in the movies. What other railroad had a popular song about it — "On the Atchison, Topeka, and the Santa Fe," from the 1944 movie, *The Harvey Girls*. The only other railroad that could boast of anything even remotely close was the Reading, for the Monopoly card that read "Take a ride on the Reading." The story of the Atchison, Topeka & Santa Fe Railway begins with the story of its route.

The Santa Fe Trail

By the mid-1600s the city of Santa Fe was well established. It was the seat of government of the Spanish colony of New Mexico and a trading center. Trade between the United States and New Mexico began in 1822, shortly after Mexico became independent from Spain. A trail was established between Independence, Missouri, just east of Kansas City, and Santa Fe. It followed the divide between the Kansas and Arkansas rivers as far west as what is now Great Bend, Kansas. From there it followed the Arkansas River west to what is now La Junta, Colorado. There it turned southwest to follow Timpas Creek toward Trinidad. The trail climbed over Raton Pass into the watershed of the Canadian River, continued southward well west of present-day Interstate Highway 25, passed through Las Vegas, then turned west to cross the Sangre de Cristo Mountains through Glorieta Pass, from which it made a quick descent to the valley of Rio Grande at Santa Fe.

The route over Raton Pass was steep and difficult, but there was water along the way and there was less danger from Indians than on other routes. In 1866 R. L. Wootton opened a toll road over the pass, making travel somewhat easier. A branch of the Santa Fe trail, the Cimarron or Dry Route, diverged to the southwest near Dodge City and followed the valley of the Cimarron River, then crossed what are now the Kiowa and Comanche National Grasslands, somewhat north of the route later used by U. S. Highway 56. The route avoided the mountains farther west, but the second name of the route explains in a word one of its two drawbacks — the other was hostile Indians. Another branch of the trail forked southward east of La Junta, passed through Branson, Colorado, and Folsom, New Mexico, and met the Cimarron Branch near Springer.

Topeka to Atchison, Topeka to Santa Fe

The Atchison & Topeka Railroad was chartered in 1859 to join the towns of its title and continue southwest toward Santa Fe. "Santa Fe" was added to the corporate name in 1863. Construction started southward from Topeka (in the opposite direction from Atchison) to tap nearby coal mines in 1869, but by early 1872 the road extended from Atchison through Topeka to Wichita. The main line west from Newton to the Kansas-Colorado state line was completed later that year.

The railroad temporarily set aside its goal of Santa Fe and continued building west along the Arkansas River. It reached Pueblo, Colorado, in 1876, just in time for the silver rush at Leadville, about 150 miles to the northwest (though the coal deposits at Canon City, a few miles west of Pueblo, were ultimately more important). In 1878 the railroad resumed construction toward Santa Fe.

Construction proceeded southwest from La Junta to Trinidad, then south over Raton Pass. The railroad was forced by geography to bypass the city of Santa Fe, which found itself at the end of a short branch from Lamy instead of astride the main line. The main line reached Albuquerque in 1880. A year later it was extended down the Rio Grande valley to meet Southern Pacific at Deming, New Mexico, forming a second railroad route across North America. In late 1882 two Santa Fe lines met at Nogales on the Sonora-Arizona border: the Sonora Railway, a Santa Fe subsidiary building north from the port of Guaymas in the Mexican state of Sonora, and a line extending southwest from Benson, Arizona, on the SP. Santa Fe was able to reach the Pacific on its own rails — except for that stretch of SP between Deming and Benson.

To the Pacific

The Atlantic & Pacific Railroad was chartered in 1866 to build west from Springfield, Missouri, along the 35th parallel of latitude (approximately through Amarillo and Albuquerque) to a junction with the Southern Pacific at the Colorado River. The A&P started construction in 1868 at Pierce City, Missouri, near Monett, and in 1871 reached Vinita, in what would become Oklahoma. By 1875 the A&P was in financial difficulty and thoroughly entangled with the ancestor of the St. Louis-San Francisco Railway (the Frisco). As an operating railroad it dropped out of sight briefly, but its charter and corporate structure remained in existence.

In 1879 the Santa Fe, the St. Louis & San Francisco, and the Atlantic & Pacific Railroad made an agreement under which AT&SF and SL&SF would jointly own and construct the A&P west from Albuquerque across New Mexico and Arizona. A provision of A&P's charter was that

Southern Pacific would build a line east from Mojave, California, to meet the A&P at the Colorado River. The A&P and the SP met at Needles, California, in 1883, and A&P leased SP's line between there and Mojave.

The Santa Fe continued to expand: a line from Barstow, California, to San Diego in 1885 and to Los Angeles in 1887; control of the Gulf, Colorado & Santa Fe (Galveston to Fort Worth) in 1886; a line between Wichita and Fort Worth in 1887; lines from Kansas City to Chicago, from Kiowa, Kansas, to Amarillo, Texas, and from Pueblo to Denver (paralleling the Denver & Rio Grande) in 1888; and purchase of the Frisco and the Colorado Midland in 1890.

During the Panic of 1893 Santa Fe entered receivership. In the subsequent reorganization the SL&SF (which Santa Fe had purchased in 1890) became independent. In 1896 the Atlantic & Pacific was split between its parents: Frisco got the portion east of Sapulpa, Oklahoma, and Santa Fe acquired the line between Albuquerque and Needles. (Congress had revoked the land grants for the portions of the line between Sapulpa and Albuquerque and west of Mojave in 1886.)

Santa Fe succeeded to the lease of the SP line from Needles to Mojave and wanted to own it in order to reach California on its own rails. The state of California wanted to break SP's monopoly in that state. In 1897 the Santa Fe traded the Sonora Railway to Southern Pacific for the SP line between Needles and Mojave, giving the Santa Fe ownership of a line all the way from Chicago to the Pacific. It was unique in that regard until the Milwaukee Road completed its extension to Puget Sound in 1909. (The Sonora Railway became the Southern Pacific of Mexico, then the Ferrocarril del Pacifico; it is now part of National Railways of Mexico.)

Latter-day expansion

Santa Fe's expansion continued: Amarillo to Pecos in 1899; Ash Fork, Arizona, to Phoenix in 1901; the Belen Cutoff from the Pecos line at Texico to Isleta, south of Albuquerque, in 1907; and the Coleman Cutoff, from Texico to Coleman, Texas, near Brownwood, in 1912.

In 1907 Santa Fe and Southern Pacific jointly formed the Northwestern Pacific Railroad, which took over several short railroads and built new lines connecting them to form a route from San Francisco north to Eureka. In 1928 Santa Fe sold its half of the NWP to Southern Pacific. Also in 1928 the Santa Fe purchased the U. S. portion of the Kansas City, Mexico & Orient (the Mexican portion of the line became the Chihuahua-Pacific Railway, now part of National Railways of Mexico). Post-World War II construction projects included an entrance to Dallas from the north and relocation of the main line across northern Arizona.

Mergers

In 1960 the Santa Fe bought the Toledo, Peoria & Western Railroad, then sold a half interest in it to the Pennsylvania Railroad. The TP&W cut straight east across Illinois from near Fort Madison, Iowa, to a connection with the Pennsylvania at Effner, Indiana, forming a bypass around

Chicago for traffic moving between the two lines. The TP&W route didn't mesh with the traffic pattern Conrail developed after 1976, so Santa Fe bought back the other half, merged the TP&W in 1983, then sold it back into independence in 1989.

Between the late 1950s and the mid-1980s the railroad scene in the United States changed drastically: freight traffic shifted from merchandise and perishables to bulk commodities, passenger railroading became a government business, and most of the large railroad companies undertook mergers that made them even larger, if fewer in number. During the 1960s the Santa Fe explored merger with the St. Louis-San Francisco and the Missouri Pacific, but neither deal got very far. Frisco became part of Burlington Northern in 1980, and the Missouri Pacific was merged by Union Pacific in 1982.

By 1980 Santa Fe, which had been the top road in route mileage in the 1950s, was surrounded by larger railroads. It was well managed and profitable, and it had the best route between the Midwest and Southern California, but its neighbors were larger and what had formerly been friendly connections were now rival railroads. Southern Pacific was in much the same situation. In 1980 Santa Fe and SP announced their merger proposal. Approval of the merger seemed certain enough that the two railroads began repainting locomotives, but in 1986 the Interstate Commerce Commission denied permission because the merger would create a monopoly. (SPSF would have been the only major railroad in New Mexico and Arizona; California would have escaped one-railroad status only by the presence of one BN route and two UP routes, all three of which use SP or Santa Fe rails for part of their route to California.)

Southern Pacific was purchased by the Denver & Rio Grande Western, and Santa Fe found itself the smallest of the Super Seven freight railroads. It began spinning off branches and secondary lines and became more than anything else a conduit for intermodal traffic — containers and trailers — between the Midwest and Southern California.

In June 1994 Santa Fe and Burlington Northern announced their intention to merge — BN would buy Santa Fe. A few months later Union Pacific made a counteroffer to purchase the Santa Fe but later dropped that offer. Approval by the Interstate Commerce Commission was complicated by the impending demise of the ICC, but the commission worked quickly and on July 20, 1995, approved the merger. As this book went to press in summer 1995 the details of the merger had not yet been made public.

Suggestions for further reading:

Santa Fe: The Railroad that Built an Empire, by James Marshall, published in 1945 by Random House, New York, New York

History of the Atchison, Topeka & Santa Fe Railway, by Keith L. Bryant, Jr., published in 1974 by Macmillan Publishing Co., Inc., 866 Third Avenue, New York, NY 10022 (ISBN 0-02-517920-9)

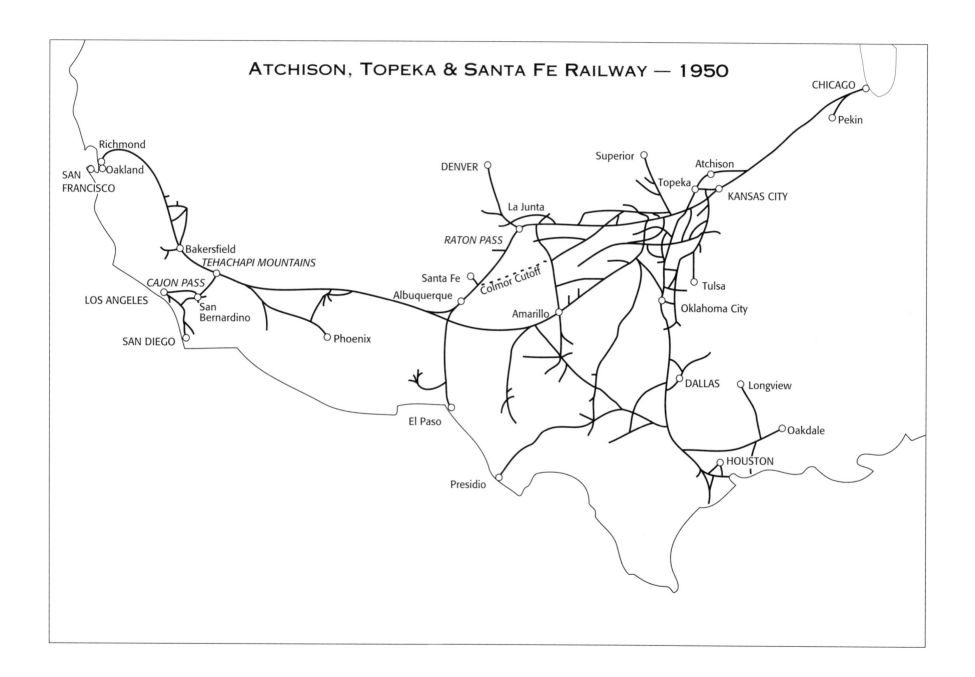

ATCHISON, TOPEKA & SANTA FE RAILWAY — 1950

During World War II the Santa Fe needed locomotives and bought three groups of secondhand steam engines: three Pennsylvania Railroad 2-8-2s, seven Boston & Maine 2-8-4s, and eight Norfolk & Western 2-8-8-2s of USRA design. Engine 1797, formerly N&W 2042, and 2-10-2 No. 3811 join forces to lift a westbound freight up the Colorado slope of Raton Pass. Photo by Preston George, April 9, 1944.

RATON PASS

For years all Santa Fe trains between the Midwest and California struggled over some of the steepest mainline grades in the United States: 6 miles of 3.5 percent grade for westbound trains (after 8 miles of 2 percent) and 7 miles of 3.3 percent for eastbounds. The climb over Raton Pass isn't a long one: 14 miles for westbound trains and 7 miles eastbound. Farther west, Santa Fe's line climbs for approximately 200 miles eastward from the Colorado River to the middle of Arizona, gaining more than 6,600 feet of elevation.

In elevation gained, Raton is a substantial climb: 1,571 feet from Trinidad to Wootton, but at Springer, New Mexico, 46 miles south of the summit, the line is nearly 200 feet lower than it was at Trinidad. For comparison, the Denver & Salt Lake climbed from 5,183 feet at Denver (the station was down near the Platte River, nearly 100 feet below the mile-high marker on the steps of the state capitol) to 11,680 feet at the summit of Rollins Pass 65, miles from Denver. Union Pacific's old line over Sherman Hill gained nearly 2,200 feet in the 31 miles west of Cheyenne. Westbound Northern Pacific trains climbed almost 2,000 feet from Whitehall, Montana, to the summit of Homestake Pass. The Pennsylvania Railroad and its successor Conrail climb 984 feet in the 11.8 miles from Altoona to Gallitzin, Pennsylvania.

Raton's distinction is steepness. Santa Fe trains travel more than 1,000 miles from Chicago to Trinidad across rolling prairie with occasional dips into river valleys. They climb more than a mile in that distance, but the climb is imperceptible. Westbound trains start climbing in earnest at Trinidad. The ruling grade is 2 percent — 2 feet per 100, 1 in 50, 105.6 feet per mile — steep by railroad standards. (Ruling grade is a grade which limits the weight of trains that can be moved over a division. It is not necessarily the steepest grade, but length is a factor — it is a stretch of grade too long for a train to be able to rely on momentum.) At Gallinas the grade becomes steeper — 3.5 percent, 184.8 feet per mile. Trains climbing the south slope of the pass are only slightly better off, with a grade of 3.3 percent, 175.3 feet per mile.

Construction

The Atchison, Topeka & Santa Fe had its first encounter with mountains in Raton Pass, on the Colorado-New Mexico state line. Santa Fe rails reached the Kansas-Colorado state line in 1872 and reached Pueblo in 1876. Already established in Pueblo was the narrow-gauge Denver & Rio Grande Railway, which was building south toward El Paso, Texas, along the eastern edge of the Rockies. D&RG's logical route south was over Raton Pass, and as a start D&RG extended its rails south to El Moro, near Trinidad.

Then the Atchison, Topeka & Santa Fe evidently remembered that it was supposed to be building toward Santa Fe. In Raton Pass there was room for only one railroad. The first company to begin constructing its line through the pass would be it. On the afternoon of February 26, 1878, D&RG and AT&SF civil engineers, unaware of each other's presence, rode south from Pueblo to El Moro on the same D&RG train. The D&RG engineers went to their hotel, intending to get an early start in the morning. The Santa Fe engineers went right to work, assisted by Trinidad residents who were angry at the D&RG for bypassing their town. (The AT&SF had political problems of its own: opposition from the territory of New Mexico.) When D&RG's crews arrived in the morning they found the Santa Fe crews already at work.

A subsequent battle with the D&RG over occupancy of the Royal Gorge of the Arkansas west of Canon City resulted in an agreement between the two roads: D&RG would relinquish its goal of El Paso and turn west into Colorado, and AT&SF would build no farther west in Colorado.

The Santa Fe began construction of the line over Raton Pass in earnest a few months later. Although work on the summit tunnel, 2,041 feet long, was progressing satisfactorily, during the last three months of 1878 the road laid out and built a temporary track over the pass so that service could begin and, just as important, construction materials could be transported west. The temporary line made backward connections at both ends of the tunnel and included four switchbacks. To cope with the 6 percent grades, the road ordered from Baldwin a 2-8-0T that was the heaviest locomotive in the world at the time (such distinctions were short-lived in those days). When the tunnel opened for service on September 1, 1879, the switchback route over the top was abandoned and dismantled. The railroad established a helper locomotive base at the south entrance of the pass at place called Willow Springs Ranch and later renamed Raton.

Improvements

Increased traffic during the 1890s prompted the Santa Fe to double-track the line over Raton Pass between 1901 and 1905. The summit tunnel severely constricted the line both because it was single track and because its cross section limited the size of cars and locomotives that could go through the tunnel. The road decided to build a second tunnel to complete its double-tracking project. The new tunnel would be parallel to the old tunnel but longer, 2,789 feet, and have a much easier grade, 0.52 percent westbound, compared to the 1.9 percent of the old tunnel. Work began in April 1907, and the new tunnel opened for service on July 9, 1908. The old tunnel remained in service for eastbound trains and was eventually enlarged and served for several decades more. Increased maintenance expenses and decreased traffic led to abandonment and plugging of the old tunnel in 1953. The 1908 tunnel continues in service today.

At the same time as it was double-tracking Raton Pass and building a new tunnel, the Santa Fe was engaged in another construction project that would have a far greater effect on traffic over Raton Pass — a route that bypassed Raton entirely. It combined existing track and new construction (the Belen Cutoff) to create a route from Newton, Kansas, southwest across Oklahoma to Amarillo, Texas, then west through Clovis and Belen, New Mexico, to a connection with the main line at Dalies, New Mexico, southwest of Albuquerque. The only major grade on the route was the climb east out of the Rio Grande valley through Abo Canyon, 40 miles and no worse than 1.25 percent. The southern route opened on July 1, 1908, and quickly became the preferred route for transcontinental freight. Most passenger trains remained on the original route over Raton Pass.

The Colmor Cutoff

Even after the Belen Cutoff was completed, the Santa Fe considered still other ways to bypass Raton Pass. In 1910 it surveyed a line along the Cimarron Cutoff of the Santa Fe Trail, from Dodge City southwest through Elkhart, Kansas, Boise City, Oklahoma, and Clayton and Farley, New Mexico, to a junction with the main line at Colmor, New Mexico, between Springer and Wagon Mound. The new route would have grades of less than 1 percent and would be 69 miles shorter than the route over Raton Pass.

Track was constructed as far as Elkhart in 1912 to tap a wheat-growing area. It was extended across the Oklahoma panhandle to Felt in 1925, and to Farley, New Mexico, in 1931, using Colorado & Southern rails between Clayton and Mount Dora, New Mexico. There remained a 35-mile gap across open country. The Depression was not a time to carry out such construction. Drought and dust killed what little business there was along the new line — a weekly mixed train was sufficient for traffic. The track already in place would have required upgrading to mainline standards, and the 35-mile gap included a crossing of the Canadian River that would have required a large bridge. Moreover, the Colmor Cutoff wouldn't have bypassed the grades of Glorieta Pass. In 1941 the Interstate Commerce Commission let the Santa Fe postpone completion of the cutoff to 1944 — and in 1942 the road abandoned the Boise City-Farley section of the line.

Note

Geographically Raton is south and slightly east of Trinidad, but the railroad direction is west. In these pages railroad directions are used for trains and tracks and compass directions for geographical features.

Suggestions for further reading:

Santa Fe's Raton Pass, by Jared V. Harper, published in 1983 by Kachina Press, 3202 Urban Avenue, Dallas, TX 75227 (ISBN 0-930724-09-7)

"The Colmor Cut-off," by Edward Mahoney, in the *NRHS Bulletin*, Volume 41, No. 1

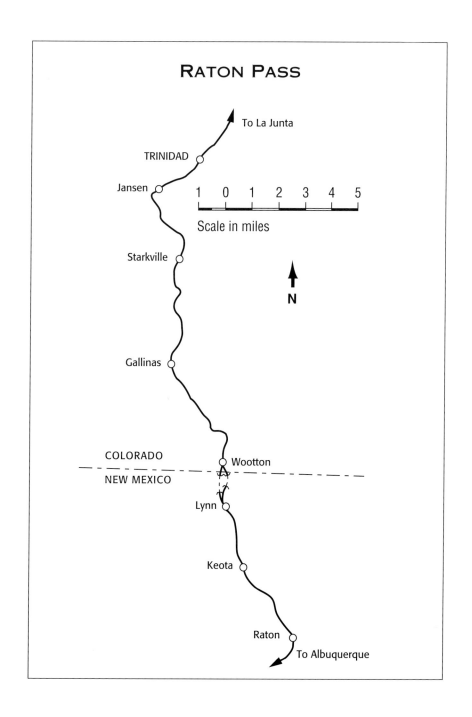

RATON PASS

To La Junta

TRINIDAD

Jansen

1 0 1 2 3 4 5

Scale in miles

N

Starkville

Gallinas

COLORADO

Wootton

NEW MEXICO

Lynn

Keota

Raton

To Albuquerque

Santa Fe was an early user of diesels in passenger service: boxcabs 1 and 1A and eight E1s plus three E1 booster units. In 1945 Santa Fe tried one of its 5400 horsepower FT freight diesels, No. 167, in passenger service. It is shown in blue and yellow freight colors lifting *El Capitan* out of Trinidad. The road reassigned ten more four-unit sets to passenger service, regearing them for 95 mph and installing steam generators, so they could heat and cool passenger trains (Santa Fe preferred steam ejector air conditioning). Photo by Lucius Beebe, November 19, 1945.

Sister 161, in red and silver passenger livery and sporting a second headlight mounted in the nose door, is in charge of train 19, the *Chief*, at Starkville. Photo by Preston George, May 18, 1946.

El Capitan began Chicago-Los Angeles service in February 1938 as a twice-weekly, extra-fare coach streamliner. Train 21 is shown at Starkville and Wootton, with 2-10-2 920, one of the first group of that type, assisting the 1800 horsepower E1 up the pass. At Starkville the photographer estimated the train was moving at 35 mph; by Wootton the 3.5 percent grade had brought the train down to 15 mph, making it a relatively easy matter to overtake the train on the parallel highway. Photos by R. H. Kindig, June 1938.

In 1948 *El Capitan* grew to a 14-car daily train, and the motive power was a four-unit set of EMD F3s. Engine 17 is carrying green flags to indicate a following second section of train 21 as it ascends near Wootton. Photo by R. H. Kindig, June 17, 1950.

Train 19, the *Chief,* ascends Raton Pass behind 2-10-2 No. 3828 and a three-unit set of F7s. The heavyweight baggage-bar-lounge car and the two New York Central sleeping cars directly behind it place the photo in 1949 or 1950. *Trains* Magazine photo by Al Rung.

PASSENGER TRAINS

All the photos of passenger trains seem to be of the same trains — the *Chief, El Capitan,* and the westbound *Super Chief.* A look at the schedules quickly yields a reason. In June 1941, for example, train 19, the *Chief,* was due out of Trinidad daily at 9 a.m. On Wednesdays and Saturdays, train 21, *El Capitan,* was 9 minutes behind the *Chief,* and train 17, the *Super Chief* was 1 hour 35 minutes behind *El Cap.* Train 3, the *California Limited,* passed through about dawn and train 7, the *Fast Mail,* about sunset — and there's not much light available for photography at dawn and sunset. The only eastbound trains during daylight were train 22, *El Capitan,* which left Raton at 12:27 p.m. Wednesdays and Saturdays, and train 20, the *Chief,* out of Raton at 2:15 p.m. daily. Ascending trains are more interesting subjects for photography because of the smoke from the steam engines. Engines on descending trains don't emit great clouds of smoke, and the train itself is often obscured by brake-shoe smoke.

Many of these photos are in sequences — train approaching, train closer, engine going away, helper approaching, helper going away — much as you would watch a train approach, pass, and disappear. Photo sequences aren't plentiful in the photo files, and they seem to be limited to low-speed mountain railroading — in other words, there was plenty of time for the photographer to turn the film-winding knob, and there wasn't much else to do while the train was passing except get another shot or two.

The *Super Chief*, train 17, ascends past the stock chute at the Wootton ranch with 2-10-2s 926 and 1651 assisting a two-unit E6. AT&SF photo.

The Budd-built streamlined *Super Chief* made its first revenue departure from Chicago on May 17, 1937. A day later it climbed Raton Pass with 2-10-2 925 helping the road engines, Santa Fe's own boxcab No. 1A and Electro-Motive demonstrator No. 512. (E1s 2 and 2A had burned out a traction motor and blown a piston during a press run a few days earlier.) Photo by Otto C. Perry, May 18, 1937.

The 12-car consist of *El Capitan* required the combined efforts of two-unit E3 No. 11 and 2-10-2s 3873 and 3811 to ascend Raton. Photo by Preston George, May 19, 1946.

The *Super Chief* and *El Capitan* began life behind diesel power; the *Chief* remained behind steam through World War II. Here it moves up the pass behind 2-8-8-2 1793, a former Norfolk & Western engine, and 4-8-4 3782. AT&SF photo, April 9, 1944.

Santa Fe lettering on the tender can't hide such N&W traits as the horizontal-bar pilot and the round-topped tender tank and the characteristically USRA shape of the cab. Instead of hopper cars of coal bound for tidewater at Norfolk are the two diesel units and 12 cars of *El Capitan* just below Wootton. Photo by Preston George, April 9, 1944.

The *Navajo*, train 9, behind 2-10-2 1704 and 4-8-2 3716, heads into the siding at Wootton to let the following *Chief* overtake it. Photo by R. H. Kindig, June 1938.

THE 2-10-2 TYPE

In 1902 the Atchison, Topeka & Santa Fe bought three 2-10-0s for use as pushers over Raton Pass. They worked well as pushers; the problem was getting them down the grade to assist the next train. There was no way to turn them at the summit; they had to back down. Their relatively long rigid wheelbase didn't take well to the curves of the line, so the Santa Fe ordered its next batch of 10-drivered engines with a rear guiding axle, creating a new wheel arrangement. The design was successful — Santa Fe bought 192 of the type between 1903 and 1913. The type was named Santa Fe.

They had a wide firebox over the rear drivers; the purpose of the trailing truck was not to make possible a larger firebox but to guide the locomotive into curves when it was running in reverse. In 1912 the Chicago, Burlington & Quincy bought five 2-10-2s that were considerably larger, the first of the wheel arrangement to have the firebox entirely behind the drivers and supported by the trailing truck. That configuration became the norm for the 2-10-2. The Santa Fe bought 140 2-10-2s of that type between 1919 and 1927. They became the standard mainline freight locomotive. They were numbered from 3800 to 3940 (3829 was an experimental 2-10-4).

By the end of World War I the 2-10-2 was the state-of-the-art heavy freight locomotive, but it had drawbacks, mostly matters of compromise. Large drive wheels created a long rigid wheelbase; small drive wheels restricted speed. Heavy main rods were necessary to withstand the piston thrust but were almost impossible to counterbalance. The forces created by the pistons were too great for fabricated mainframes; cast frames were still in the future.

Engine 972, built in 1904 and pictured in 1941, illustrates the earlier configuration of the 2-10-2 type, with the firebox positioned over the rear pair of drivers and the trailing truck primarily serving as a guiding axle when the locomotive is operated in reverse. Engine 3864, built in 1923 and pictured in 1939, is of the later type, with a deeper firebox carried behind the drive wheels and supported by the trailing truck. Both photos by F. J. Peterson.

After 1908 transcontinental freight moved on the easier southern route through Amarillo, Texas, and Belen, New Mexico. Only local traffic and through freights between Colorado or western Kansas and the West used the route over Raton Pass. Three 2-10-2s, Nos. 1645 and 3928 on the head and No. 3904 pushing behind the caboose, have a 56-car freight moving up the pass near Wootton. Photos by R. H. Kindig, June 18, 1950.

FT No. 161 in passenger "Warbonnet" livery leads the *Chief* upgrade at Wootton. Carrying the drumhead sign is observation-sleeper *Denehotso*. Both photos by R. H. Kindig, May 18, 1946.

Two helpers and 4-8-4 No. 3769 lead the westbound *Chief* into the newer of the two tunnels at the summit of Raton Pass. The sign between the tracks next to the sleeper ahead of the observation car reads "Lower Extended Stack." AT&SF photos.

By April 1953 searchlight signals had replaced semaphores at Wootton and the old tunnel had been abandoned. Engine 3913, a 2-10-2, on the head end takes a 34-car freight into the summit tunnel with the assistance of a sister 2-10-2, No. 3898, on the rear. The little obelisk just in front of the tunnel portal marks the Colorado-New Mexico state line. Photos by Philip R. Hastings, April 1953.

Two 2-10-2s, 3874 and 3873, work hard to lift eastbound freight through Lynn. The engineer of the lead engine can see the summit of the pass ahead, though the portal of the eastbound tunnel is out of sight around the curve. Pushing hard on the rear of the same train are two more 2-10-2s, 936 and 3875. AT&SF photos, 1946.

An ex-Norfolk & Western 2-8-8-2, No. 1797, assists 4-8-4 No. 3777 with the 14 cars of the eastbound *Chief*, train 20, just below Lynn. Bringing up the rear is sleeper-observation car *Biltabito*, built by Pullman in 1938. Photos by Preston George, April 9, 1944.

Two 2-10-2s assist the eastbound *Chief*'s 4-8-4 up the south slope of the pass at Keota. Winter sunlight glints off the curved end of the observation car. AT&SF photos.

At the same place in June 1951 a freight drifts down the grade behind 2-10-2s 3822 and 3828. A bit later that same day oil-burning 2-10-2 No. 3807 shoves on the rear of an eastbound freight. All-steel construction permits positioning the helper behind the caboose. Photos by George C. Corey.

Train 22, the all-coach, extra-fare *El Capitan*, climbs the south slope of the pass at Keota, with 2-10-2 1695 and 2-10-4 5000 helping two-unit E6 No. 15. Photos by Preston George.

An eastbound freight ascends the pass with two 2-10-2s, 1651 and 3823, pulling and two more, 1703 and 901, pushing on the rear. In the first photo the through truss bridge that carries the highway over the railroad at the north edge of Raton is visible just ahead of the exhausts of the two pushers; in the distance is the open country south of Raton. The third photo (page 50) is at Keota, as is the fourth (page 51), showing the helpers returning to Raton in reverse. Photos by E. C. Storm, July 1949.

A 12-car *El Capitan* is doing 20 mph at Keota with the combined efforts of two-unit E6 No. 12 and 2-10-2 No. 934 on Memorial Day, 1942. The hood on the headlight of the diesel confirms the World War II date. Photo by R. H. Kindig.

The second section of train 8, the *Fast Mail*, is about to pass under the highway bridge a mile out of Raton. On the point is 4-8-4 No. 3764; pushing at the rear is a 2-10-2. Photo by Preston George, May 18, 1946.

Engine 926, one of Santa Fe's first group of 2-10-2s, awaits assignment at Raton. Beyond is Raton's mission-style passenger station. Photo by Ross B. Grenard, March 26, 1949.

Raton's engine terminal had a large roundhouse, about three-quarters of a circle. The tall steel water tank beyond engine 926 was typical of the Santa Fe. The Fairbanks-Morse coaling towers in the foreground date from 1934; 2-8-8-2 No. 1797 barely visible beyond them puts a World War II date on this photo. AT&SF photo.

Not long afterward engine service became a matter of water hoses at the ends of the passenger platform, for cleaning the windshield and filling the boiler water tanks. Santa Fe passenger cars required steam year-round, for heat in the winter and air conditioning in the summer. Photo by E. C. Storm, July 1949.

Mikado 4010 leads new four-unit F7 225 (note the shine on the nose of the diesel) on a 110-car train of refrigerator cars. Pushing on the rear are another Mikado, No. 4009, and 2-10-2 No. 3844. Photo by Stan Kistler, June 17, 1950.

Cajon Pass

The Mediterranean climate of the Los Angeles Basin is a product of the Pacific Ocean to the west and mountain ranges to the north, east, and south. The mountains not only restrict the passage of weather patterns but also make access to the Los Angeles Basin difficult. Even today the major highways follow the same routes the railroads used. (The one major route that does not follow a railroad is I-5 from the north, which follows practically a straight line from Bakersfield to Los Angeles, making a direct attack on the Tehachapi Mountains — a route the Santa Fe considered from time to time.)

The first rail route in and out of Los Angeles was Southern Pacific's original line from Mojave through Soledad Canyon and the San Fernando Valley, then east through Colton and over San Gorgonio Pass to Indio, Yuma, and eventually New Orleans. State Highway 14 follows that route from Mojave to San Fernando; I-10 follows the SP route east from Los Angeles.

Southern Pacific's Coast Route from San Francisco and Santa Barbara enters the San Fernando Valley through Santa Susana Pass. It is paralleled by State Highway 118, the Simi Valley Freeway.

Santa Fe's Surf Line along the coast from San Diego turns inland from the coast north of San Clemente because of the precipitous cliffs along the coast north of there. I-5, the Santa Ana and San Diego Freeways, follows that same route.

The only practical route from the northeast is Cajon Pass, used first by the Santa Fe, then Union Pacific, and in relatively recent times by Southern Pacific. I-15 follows the railroad over Cajon, then exits the Los Angeles Basin using much the same route as Santa Fe's first attempt to connect San Diego with the east.

Cajon Pass is a gap between the San Gabriel and San Bernardino mountain ranges, which form the north rim of the Los Angeles Basin. North of the mountains is the upper part of the Mojave Desert, lying at an altitude of about 3,000 feet. The south side of the pass takes the form of a canyon running northwest from San Bernardino (at 1,077 feet), climbing gradually for about 10 miles, then more steeply (and paralleling the San Andreas Fault). The canyon turns to the northeast for a mile through Blue Cut, crosses the fault, then resumes its northwesterly course and becomes even steeper to Summit (3,823 feet). The north side of the pass is a relatively gentle ascent across the desert from Victorville (2,714 feet).

A toll wagon road was built through Cajon Pass in 1860, and in the 1870s the pass was surveyed for the Los Angeles & Independence Railroad, which aimed to connect Santa Monica, west of Los Angeles, with the silver-mining area in the Owens Valley. A short portion of the railroad was built from Santa Monica to Los Angeles, and a tunnel at the summit of the pass was begun. About 1875 mining and banking reversals caused the cessation of all work on the LA&I. Southern Pacific eventually acquired the road and its right-of-way in Cajon Pass.

Southern Pacific

This book is about the Santa Fe, not the Southern Pacific, but it is impossible to discuss the history of railroads in California without bringing in SP and its ancestor, Central Pacific. It was a California company. It built eastward, not westward, to connect California with the rest of the United States. It held a virtual monopoly on transportation in California well into the 20th century, and it was a major force in California politics. Its abuses of power earned it widespread hatred. It has had a hard time living down the reputation it gained in its youth.

Southern Pacific had a charter to build south along the coast from San Francisco to San Diego, then east. Central Pacific acquired SP in 1870, a year after it met the Union Pacific at Promontory, Utah, then started building south through the San Joaquin Valley under the provisions of SP's charter. The line reached Bakersfield in 1874, then crossed the Tehachapi Mountains into the Mojave Desert. SP intended to continue directly southeast via Cajon Pass to the Colorado River at Yuma, Arizona, but was induced to detour south to Los Angeles before turning east. (In the 1960s SP built a cutoff through Cajon Pass so through freight traffic could bypass the congestion of Los Angeles.)

California Southern

Santa Fe's efforts to reach the Pacific came head to head with Southern Pacific. The California Southern Railroad, a Santa Fe subsidiary, was chartered in 1880 to build north from San Diego to

Barstow, between Needles and Mojave. Construction progressed up the coast to Oceanside (throughout this book present-day place names are used), then inland through Fallbrook and Temecula Canyon. By mid-1882 the line was in operation as far north as Colton on the Southern Pacific. SP refused to allow the Santa Fe line to cross its line, but Santa Fe leapfrogged ahead and built 4 more miles of track from Colton to San Bernardino. A minor railroad war ensued, and ultimately Santa Fe installed a crossing. In September 1882 the line was placed in service between San Diego and San Bernardino.

Floods in February 1883 washed out the line in Temecula Canyon. Santa Fe abandoned the line through the canyon and built a new one (opened in 1888) through San Juan Capistrano, Orange, and Corona, leaving stubs of the old line in place from Oceanside to Fallbrook and Temecula to Colton.

Soon after work stopped on the Los Angeles & Independence Railroad, the California Southern surveyed another route through the Cajon Pass. The CS route was east of the LA&I. It required heavier construction toward the summit but no tunnel, and its summit was at a considerably lower summit elevation. Construction began in 1881, then stopped, then resumed in 1885. The line was completed in November of that year.

In 1887 Santa Fe completed a line between San Bernardino and Los Angeles via Pasadena and a year later opened another line into Los Angeles from Orange. In 1889 Santa Fe combined the California Southern and the California Central (San Bernardino to Los Angeles) to form the Southern California Railway, which became part of the Santa Fe in 1904. The Atlantic & Pacific became the Santa Fe Pacific Railroad in 1898; that became part of the Santa Fe in 1903.

Grades and track

The line over Cajon pass climbed out of San Bernardino on a 2.2 percent grade. At Cajon, about 19 miles from San Bernardino, the grade increased to 3 percent; it continued at 3 percent to Summit, 25.4 miles from San Bernardino. The westbound ascending grade was far less severe. From Barstow (elevation 2,105 feet) to Victorville (2,714 feet) the line followed the Mojave River with a maximum grade of 0.72 percent; from Victorville to Summit the maximum grade is 1.6 percent.

The 3 percent grade in the upper part of the pass was an undeniable operating handicap, and traffic soon required a second track. In the early 1900s the Santa Fe surveyed a route 2 miles longer that maintained a 2.2 percent grade all the way to the summit. The second track on the west side of the pass was constructed between 1910 and 1913. It became the eastbound (uphill) track, but because it lay to the north of the original line (west by the compass), left-hand operation became the rule. The line between Summit and Barstow was double-tracked between 1910 and 1924 with the new track adjacent to the old. Between Hesperia and Victorville the new second track swung away from the old, made an S curve, and crossed the old line on a bridge, restoring right-hand operation between there and Barstow.

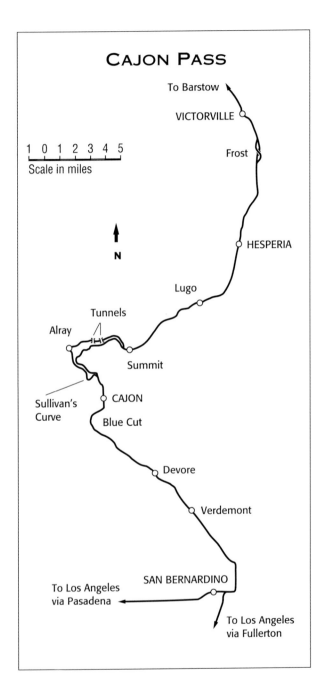

CAJON PASS

To Barstow
VICTORVILLE
Frost
HESPERIA
Lugo
Tunnels
Alray
Summit
Sullivan's
Curve
CAJON
Blue Cut
Devore
Verdemont
SAN BERNARDINO
To Los Angeles
via Pasadena
To Los Angeles
via Fullerton

1 0 1 2 3 4 5
Scale in miles

N

Union Pacific

Union Pacific's route from Salt Lake City to Los Angeles was opened in 1905 as the San Pedro, Los Angeles & Salt Lake Railroad. It was the product of a merger of two competing projects: an extension of UP's Oregon Short Line southwest from Salt Lake City and William Clark's proposal for a railroad from southern California northeast into Nevada and Utah. Numerous routes were surveyed into and out of the Los Angeles Basin, but Cajon Pass was the only logical route. UP wanted to avoid unnecessary construction and asked Santa Fe for trackage rights between Colton, just south of San Bernardino, and Daggett, 9 miles east of Barstow. The two roads reached agreement — after two years of negotiation — only days before UP inaugurated service, and the initial contract was for only three years.

In the Department of What Might Have Been, had Santa Fe not granted trackage rights, UP might have utilized the Los Angeles & Independence survey (UP controlled SP, which had bought the LA&I) and built its own line. Ultimately, instead of Santa Fe's double-tracking project, the two roads might have operated their lines as paired track — UP in one direction and Santa Fe in the other.

Footnote

As with Raton Pass, railroad and geographic directions are at odds. From Barstow trains that are westbound by the timetable run more or less south by the compass to the summit of Cajon Pass, where they turn southeast for the descent to San Bernardino, then turn west again. Train directions are given according to the timetable; geographic features are described by compass direction.

Suggestions for further reading:

Chard Walker's Cajon — Rail Passage to the Pacific, by Chard L. Walker, published in 1985 by Trans-Anglo Books, P. O. Box 94911, Pasadena, CA 91109 (ISBN 0-87046-072-2)

Chard Walker's Cajon — A Pictorial Album, by Chard L. Walker, published in 1990 by Trans-Anglo Books, P. O. Box 94911, Pasadena, CA 91109 (ISBN 0-87046-095-1)

In a rare instance of engines of both roads being used on a train, Santa Fe 4-8-2 No. 3725 and Union Pacific 4-6-6-4 No. 3939 lead the westbound *Los Angeles Challenger* through Ono. Photo by R. H. Kindig, November 1, 1941.

An all-streamlined *Chief*, train 20, rolls upgrade past Cajon station in the rain behind 2-10-2 No. 3928 and 4-8-4 No. 3770. Photo by Ed. W. Bewley.

Orange-sided refrigerator cars hang on the drawbar of 2-10-2 No. 1677, built in 1912, just above Cajon station. Between 1677 and two newer 2-10-2s pushing on the rear, 3896 and 3866, are 86 cars. Photo by Stan Kistler, June 11, 1949.

The heaviest 4-8-4s were Santa Fe's 2900 class, built by Baldwin in 1943 and 1944 — heavy to begin with and heavier because of wartime restrictions on materials. Engine 2916 rolls downgrade with the second section of train 23, the *Grand Canyon*. Photo by Robert Hale, November 11, 1951.

The combined drawbar pulls of a 2-10-2 and a 4-8-4 — engines 1675 and 3758 — lift the eastbound *Grand Canyon* up the pass. Photo by Herb Sullivan.

PASSENGER TRAINS

As on Raton Pass, the passenger-train pictures are mostly of the same trains, and for the same reason. Most passenger trains went over Cajon Pass by night. In 1942 trains 3, the *California Limited*, and 19, the *Chief*, descended to San Bernardino right after breakfast; 20, the eastbound *Chief*, and 22, *El Capitan*, left San Bernardino between 1 and 2 p.m.

In 1946 several westbound trains descended just before and after sunrise: 1, the *Scout*; 3, the *California Limited*; 17, on alternate days the *Super Chief* and *El Capitan*; and 19, the *Chief*. The *Grand Canyon*, train 23, came down midafternoon and 7, the *Fast Mail*, just before sunset. The eastbound *Grand Canyon*, train 24, left San Bernardino at 11 a.m. and the eastbound *Chief* at 1:45 p.m. In 1949 the *Grand Canyon* arrived San Bernardino from the east at 8:40 a.m. and train 7, the *Fast Mail*, at 4:55 p.m. The eastbound *Chief*, *Grand Canyon*, and *El Capitan* all climbed the pass in midafternoon.

In 1953 the two sections of the *Grand Canyon*, trains 123 and 23, reached San Bernardino at 8:25 and 8:40 a.m. and the *Fast Mail* arrived at 3:55 p.m. There were four trains in the midafternoon eastbound parade: train 20, the *Chief*; 22, *El Capitan*; and 24 and 124, the two sections of the *Grand Canyon*.

Between Cajon station and Sullivan's Curve the north track cuts through a ridge of sandstone. Three eastbound freights powered by the ubiquitous 2-10-2s forward, mid-train, and on the rear are shown where the line slices through the rock — one of the few stretches of straight track in the upper part of the pass. Three photos by Herb Sullivan.

The same place was the location for a runby for a Los Angeles-Barstow excursion operated by the Railway Club of Southern California. The road engine is 4-8-4 No. 2929; the helper is No. 3841, a 2-10-2. Equipment for the train was a spare set of *El Capitan* equipment. Photo by Stan Kistler, November 26, 1950.

Freight drifts downhill behind engine 3879, a 2-10-2. The feather of steam from the safety valve indicates the engine isn't using much steam, and the brake-shoe smoke along the train testifies to the grade. Photo by Robert Hale.

Herb Sullivan's photos of 1905-vintage Pacific 1226 assisting the E units (in these photos E1A No. 6 and an E6B) of *El Capitan* have become a cliche — because they are dramatic photos. Sullivan's patience in returning to the same spot for the same train (and *El Capitan* ran twice-weekly in those days) is evident in these three photos. The train consist is the same but there's a difference in smoke — it could be a matter of the skill of the fireman or a request made by the photographer for ample smoke — and there are differences in such details as cab awning, diesel windshield wipers, and shades in the car windows.

HERB SULLIVAN AND SULLIVAN'S CURVE

Herb Sullivan was born February 25, 1887, in Emerson, Manitoba. In 1903 his family moved to Porterville, California, where his father acquired orange groves; later the family moved to southern California and bought orange groves in Placentia, northeast of Anaheim. Sullivan wanted to work for a railroad, but his mother was opposed to that because of the dangers of the job. After graduating from high school Sullivan studied photography; during World War I he was engaged in aerial photography until he was summoned home to take over management of the orange groves for his father, who had fallen ill. Sullivan's interest in railroads continued, and he became a member of several railroad clubs. His favorite photo location was Cajon Pass, and in the pass, at a curve on the north (eastbound) track near a pair of enormous sandstone rock formations. The place was informally named Sullivan's Curve; in the 1960s the U. S. Forestry Service gave the name official status. Sullivan died in May 1945.

A slightly more distant view of the *Chief* swinging around Sullivan's Curve behind 4-8-4 No. 3768 shows the size of the rock formation there. Photo by Herb Sullivan.

Pacific 1226 and Northern 3760 lift train 24, the *Grand Canyon*, up the pass at Sullivan's Curve. Photo by Herb Sullivan.

Pacific 1226 appears again on the *Grand Canyon*, this time ahead of engine 3758. A few Pullman passengers are enjoying the view from the observation platform. Photo by Herb Sullivan.

OPERATIONS

There were several interesting quirks of operations in Cajon Pass. Until 1948 the most restrictive signal an eastbound train could encounter between Highland Junction and Summit was a single yellow light. Such a signal indicated that the next block was occupied but permitted trains to keep moving at restricted speed ready to stop short of a preceding train. On the steep ascending grade, closing the throttle was just as effective as applying the brakes to stop the train, but the lack of true stop signals meant that trains rarely had to stop and then start again on the grade. In 1948 the sequence of aspect was changed from green, yellow over yellow, and yellow to green, yellow, and red over yellow. In 1953 the system was again changed to include a stop-and-proceed indication, but a plate with the letter "G" (for grade) on the signal mast allows trains to pass a red signal without stopping.

Water was available for eastbound trains at Keenbrook, 15 miles out of San Bernardino, and Cajon, 3.7 miles farther. At Keenbrook water columns were located at both ends of the siding, so the road engine and the helper on the rear could take water, if not simultaneously, at least without having to move the train much. If a train stopped so the pusher could take water, the road engine could uncouple, move ahead, fill its tender, then back down onto the train. On the east slope, water was available at Victorville. No water was available at Summit on the assumption that engines needing water could drift downgrade without using much additional water to Keenbrook, Cajon, or Victorville. Water for domestic use at Summit was brought in by tank car. Diesels, of course, could omit the water stops.

Westbound trains were required to stop for a brake test at Summit, and freight trains were required to stop for 10 minutes at Cajon and Devore to let their wheels cool (in later years the use of dynamic brakes obviated the need for such stops).

Cajon Pass was helper territory — rare indeed was the train that ventured out of San Bernardino without a second engine. Passenger trains had the helper up front; freight trains usually had their helpers pushing on the rear just ahead of the caboose. At Summit freight helpers uncoupled from the train, backed the caboose into inclined track, and pulled ahead out of the way. The train crew then released the brakes to let the caboose roll forward and couple to the train. Midtrain helpers were harder to cut in and out.

Freight trains almost always got 2-10-2s as helpers. There was a little more variety in passenger helpers: 4-6-2 No. 1226 was a regular passenger helper, and helper duties were sometimes assumed by 4-6-4s and 4-4-2s, wheel arrangements not usually thought of in connection with helper service.

Cajon Pass was not high-speed territory until recent years. Eastbound trains ascending the pass were limited not by timetable restrictions but by the power of the locomotives. In 1942, just before the advent of diesel locomotives with dynamic brakes, westbound freight trains were limited to 15 mph from Summit down to Cajon — expressed as 4 minutes per mile — and 20 mph from Cajon to San Bernardino. Eastbound freights were held to 24 mph from Summit to Hesperia. Westbound passenger trains were restricted to 30 mph from Summit to Cajon and to 22 mph from Cajon to Keenbrook — a minimum of 40 minutes from Summit to San Bernardino. Nowadays westbound freights are limited to 20 mph from Summit to Cajon and westbound passenger trains to 30 mph. Eastbound trains are limited to 30 mph in that territory because of curves — and locomotive power has increased enough in recent decades that it is necessary to post speed limits for trains moving uphill.

Santa Fe type No. 1621, built by Baldwin in 1905, works upgrade around the curve with empty stock cars behind its tender. Photo by Herb Sullivan.

Santa Fe posed its first road freight diesel, blue-and-yellow FT 100, at Sullivan's Curve, with a train of nicely matched, clean refrigerator cars and box cars, soon after the diesel was delivered. AT&SF photo, 1941.

The pictorial emphasis was obviously on the helper, 2-10-2 No. 3839, assisting E6A No. 13 and an E1B, on *El Capitan*. Photo by William Barham, March 10, 1946.

The *Grand Canyon*, train 24, approaches the top of the pass behind Pacific 1226 and Northern 3761. The 10-car train is doing about 20 mph. Photo by F. J. Peterson, July 10, 1940.

Pacific 1226 forsakes its usual role as a passenger helper to take a 13-car freight extra up the pass unassisted — it is shown in the broad upper reaches of the pass. Most of the cars are empty gondolas, but on the rear are four flat cars carrying heavy artillery. Photo by R. H. Kindig, June 21, 1946.

The usual helper engine on Cajon Pass was a 2-10-2, and Pacific 1226 had an extended tour of duty as a passenger helper. Occasionally exotic power appeared. Pacific 1376, streamlined (along with 1369) in 1939 for the *Valley Flyer*, assists 4-8-4 No. 3755 with the *Grand Canyon*. Photo by H. H. Halton, October 1941.

Hudson 3459, borrowed from the Valley Division, teams up with 2901 on a Shrine convention special running as the third section of train 123, the *Grand Canyon*, near Victorville. Photo by Stan Kistler, June 18, 1950.

The eastbound *Chief* nears the summit with 2-10-2 No. 3855 and 4-8-4 No. 3776 on the head end. The west-bound track, the original line, is visible at the left edge of the picture. Photo by F. J. Peterson, October 16, 1945.

An eastbound freight has just passed Alray siding with engine 972, a Baldwin product of 1903, cut in ahead of a wood-bodied caboose. Photo by R. H. Kindig, November 1, 1941.

Not far out of San Bernardino Pacific 1226 and Mountain 3727 have train 10, the *Navajo*, rolling at 35 mph. Photo by R. H. Kindig, October 11, 1939.

With its stack fully extended, engine 2905, one of Santa Fe's wartime group of Northerns, swings through the reverse curves at Devore with the second section of the *Grand Canyon*. The big 4-8-4 is now in helper service after less than a decade as a road locomotive — the train's diesels are barely visible behind the enormous 16-wheel tender. Photo by Robert Hale, December 2, 1951.

Two 4-8-4s, 2923 and 3776, are in charge of an eastbound Shrine convention special about a mile west of Summit. Photo by Jim Ady, June 1950.

The second — coach — section of train 24, the *Grand Canyon*, works up the pass behind
4-8-4 No. 2929. Photo by Jim Ady, September 1948.

Train 22, the eastbound *El Capitan*, swings around the final curve into Summit after climbing from San Bernardino. The south track (the original line) can be seen diverging above the next-to-last car of the train. Photo by Robert Hale, February 1951.

Two freights, both behind blue-and-yellow F7s, meet on the curve just west of Summit. Photo by Robert Hale.

The railroad facilities at Summit included a station, a collection of smaller buildings and shed, a stock pen, east-bound and westbound sidings, and a wye for turning helpers. Visible at the left edge of the photo is the former Los Angeles Railway funeral car *Descanso*, which was moved to Summit in 1940 by the Railroad Boosters and used as a bunkhouse. The community's water was brought from Victorville weekly in the tank car spotted near the wye. The second section of the westbound *Grand Canyon* is shown passing a westbound freight. Visible at the door of the depot is Chard Walker, for years the operator there. Photo by Robert Hale, December 2, 1951.

The heaviest 4-8-4s were Santa Fe's 2900 class, two of which are shown leading train 24, the *Grand Canyon*, into Summit. Photo by Chard Walker.

Summit was often a busy place. Left to right are an eastbound freight with a two-unit helper to be cut out, a westbound freight in the siding to be overtaken by a westbound passenger train, and a cow-and-calf set of switchers, which Union Pacific used as helpers in the 1950s. Photo by Stan Kistler.

Moist air coming in from the ocean could bring fog and rain to the Los Angeles Basin, but those conditions down below could mean snow at Summit's elevation, 3,823 feet. Photo by Robert Hale.

CHARD WALKER

Chard Walker was born in Swampscott, Massachusetts, on June 8, 1922, and moved to Los Angeles with his family in 1939. In 1946 he spent a month recovering his health at Summit, and he decided he liked railroads and the high desert. He studied telegraphy and became a train-order operator for the Santa Fe, first at Victorville, then at Summit. He remained at Summit, marrying and raising a family there, until that station was closed in 1967, then worked at Barstow and Victorville until he retired in 1983.

Operator Chard Walker hands up orders to the fireman of a 2-10-2. Photo by Robert Hale, December 3, 1950.

The 9,000- to 10,000-foot summits of the San Gabriel Mountains, rarely visible from the south, tower more than a mile above the summit of the pass. Photo by Robert Hale.

Passenger trains sometimes ran in two or more sections to handle overflow loads of mail and express or special passenger movement. The second and third sections of train 19, the *Chief*, are shown near Lugo in the valley east of Summit behind Mountain type 3735 and Santa Fe type 3940. Both photos by William Barham, March 10, 1946.

Between Victorville and Hesperia the two tracks cross to prepare for left-hand running through Summit and down to San Bernardino. In the foreground is a joshua tree, a member of the yucca family. Photo by Robert Hale, February 1951.

A westbound Shrine convention special rolls west near Frost. It is running as the second section of train 23, the *Grand Canyon*, and carrying green flags to indicate another section follows. Photo by Stan Kistler, June 18, 1950.

Another Shrine convention special is shown behind 2-8-2 No. 3221 and 4-8-4 No. 2924 just west of Frost, where lefthand running begins. Photo by Stan Kistler, June 18, 1950.

A single F7 helps 2930, one of Santa Fe's big 4-8-4s, with the second section of the westbound *Grand Canyon* at Frost. Photo by Robert Hale, December 1, 1951.

A freight works west at Frost behind a pair of 2-10-2s, the second of which is the last of the class. Photo by Stan Kistler, June 11, 1949.

Joshua trees frame the Alcos of the westbound *Chief* near Victorville. Photo by Stan Kistler, June 1950.

Just west of the Victorville the railroad and the Mojave River squeeze through a short canyon known as the Upper Narrows. A four-unit set of F7s accelerates the westbound *Grand Canyon* out of Victorville. Photo by Stan Kistler.

A westbound freight with F7 No. 226 on the point crosses the Mojave River at Victorville.
Photo by Joseph J. Lynch, April 1950.

A four-unit set of FTs leads an eastbound freight upgrade out of Tunnel 10 just above Tehachapi Loop. Photo by Frank Clodfelter.

TEHACHAPI PASS

The Tehachapi Mountains are a range in south central California running east and west between the south end of the Sierra Nevada and the Coast Ranges. They form the south end of California's central valley and the northern boundary of the western part of the Mojave Desert. They are not especially high by Western standards (the highest peak is Double Mountain, 7,988 feet), but they are dry and rugged and form a barrier both geographic and cultural between the central valley and southern California. Tehachapi Pass (3,799 feet) lies at the east end of the range.

Southern Pacific

The rails over the Tehachapis are owned by Southern Pacific. Santa Fe's story here, as elsewhere in California, involves SP. The Southern Pacific Railroad was chartered in the early 1860s to build a railroad from San Francisco down the coast to San Diego, then east. When the Atlantic & Pacific was chartered in 1866, Southern Pacific's charter was amended to allow it to branch southeast through Gilroy and Tres Pinos, over Pacheco Pass into the San Joaquin Valley, then over the Tehachapis and east to the Colorado River to meet the A&P.

The San Francisco & San Jose began operation in 1864 and soon merged the Southern Pacific, at that point a paper railroad. The builders of the Central Pacific (Huntington, Hopkins, Stanford, and Crocker, known collectively as the Big Four) saw the San Francisco & San Jose as a potential competitor and bought the city of San Francisco's interest in that railroad — and along with it the Southern Pacific and its charter. They formed a new corporation, the Southern Pacific Railroad of California, in 1870.

The line south from San Jose reached Tres Pinos in 1871. Exploration showed there would be almost no local business to support a line beyond there (even today there is little on the California map between Hollister and Coalinga). Central Pacific management decided it would be wiser and easier to build a line south from some point on the Central Pacific between Sacramento and Oakland. Accordingly, construction began at Lathrop, 9 miles south of Stockton, at the end of

1869. Rails reached Modesto in less than a year; Fresno in 1872; and Sumner, on high ground across the Kern River from Bakersfield, in November 1874.

The Central Pacific built south to Goshen Junction (between Hanford and Visalia), where it encountered the line planned and surveyed by the Southern Pacific — the line that was to have been built over Pacheco Pass. Beyond Goshen Junction the new railroad was Southern Pacific.

Construction continued southeast with relatively easy grades, climbing from Sumner at 420 feet to Caliente at 1,291 feet. Caliente remained the end of track for more than a year. SP's assistant chief engineer William Hood laid out the line over Tehachapi. He started with a horseshoe curve to begin a climb out of the valley of Caliente Creek. In the 7 miles from Caliente through Bealville to Cliff the railroad climbs 702 feet and covers a net distance of little more than a mile.

The line twists in and out of side canyons to gain elevation before reaching the canyon of Tehachapi Creek. (Tehachapi Creek flows into Caliente Creek at Caliente, but the lower part of its canyon is too steep for a railroad to follow.) Above Woodford two horseshoe curves change the direction from east to west and back east again and into Tunnel 9. There the line makes a complete circle, crossing over itself and gaining 77 feet in elevation.

The loop was a way to add distance to the line to keep the grade within limits. The idea seems obvious enough now, but it wasn't when the line was built. William Hood's innovation has been used by railroads in only a few other places in North America — Canadian Pacific's spiral tunnels in Kicking Horse Pass (1908), Louisville & Nashville's Hiwassee Loop (1898), Western Pacific's Williams Loop (1909), the Bonavista branch of the Newfoundland Railway (1911), and near Creel on the Chihuahua Pacific — but it is found in many freeway interchanges.

Above the loop the line follows the west wall of the canyon of Tehachapi Creek, popping in and out of several tunnels. The top end of the canyon broadens into a valley that contains the town of Tehachapi. The grade eases as it continues to the summit, 2 miles east of Tehachapi. The total gain in elevation in the 50 miles from Bakersfield to the summit is 3,628 feet.

The 18-mile descent from the summit to Mojave is as direct as the west slope is tortuous. It begins with 8 miles of 1.16 percent descending grade east, then southeast across the floor of Tehachapi Valley. Tehachapi Pass, a gap between the Horned Toad Hills and Pajuela Peak, marks the east end of the broad valley and the beginning of a steeper descent, 2.34 percent. The line follows the canyon of Cache Creek heading east-northeast for about 6 miles, then turns 90 degrees to the south-southeast and drops down into Mojave. In the 18 miles from the summit to Mojave the line drops 1,279 feet.

Southern Pacific planned to build directly east from Mojave to the Colorado River at Needles (and eventually did so), but the young city of Los Angeles wanted to be on the railroad and induced SP to detour south through Soledad Pass and the San Fernando Valley — for about $600,000 plus the Los Angeles & San Pedro Railroad. SP continued east through Colton and Indio to the Colorado River and onward to Yuma, Tucson, and El Paso to head off the Texas & Pacific.

There is no denying that SP's line was instrumental in developing agriculture in the San Joaquin Valley. It held a monopoly on transportation there (indeed throughout California) and gained a reputation for all kinds of abuses of that monopoly. A group of merchants, farmers, and other shippers was formed to fight the SP. In 1893 the association, backed by sugar magnate Claus Spreckels, decided to construct an independent railroad down the valley from Stockton. In February 1895 the state issued a charter for the San Francisco & San Joaquin Valley Railway. The line was opened from Stockton to Fresno in October 1896; by May of 1897 it was into Bakersfield.

Southern Pacific's reaction to competition was to undercut the San Francisco & San Joaquin Valley's rates with the hope that the road would lose money and SP could purchase it at bargain rates. However, Spreckels, eager to break SP's monopoly, sold the SF&SJV to the Santa Fe, which announced it was extending its line to San Francisco.

There was the matter of the 68-mile gap between Bakersfield and Mojave. Even though SP already occupied the only feasible route over the Tehachapis, Spreckels incorporated the Bakersfield & Los Angeles Rail Road, which would include an 8,000-foot tunnel. The Santa Fe itself proposed a line over Brites Summit, directly west of present-day Tehachapi, then down into valley of Tejon Creek. It would have a 2 percent grade but certainly be no more difficult to operate than SP's line.

At that point Southern Pacific knew it couldn't prevent Santa Fe from reaching the shore of San Francisco Bay — Santa Fe's proposal was not just idle talk. SP would lose its monopoly in northern California. It could all but aim a telescope across the bay from its San Francisco headquarters and see lines of invading red-and-silver warbonnet diesels.

SP's line over the Tehachapis had been expensive to construct and was expensive to maintain — a tenant might help pay those costs. The two roads came to agreement on terms: an annual fee plus half of all taxes; maintenance crews would be employed jointly; operation would be by SP rules and with SP dispatching, but trains would receive equal treatment by class of train.

That accomplished, Santa Fe built west from Stockton to San Francisco Bay at Richmond. There too SP had already taken the best route; Santa Fe had to cope with the swamps of the San Joaquin Delta and unstable soil in the hills between Martinez and Richmond. Passenger service to Richmond (with a ferry from Richmond to San Francisco) began July 6, 1900.

Operations

The line between Bakersfield and Mojave quickly became one of the busiest single-track mountain railroads in the world. Southern Pacific's Coast Line between Los Angeles and San Francisco, opened in 1901, took little freight traffic away from the Tehachapi route — the Coast Line was principally a passenger route.

Freight traffic over Tehachapi increased rapidly with the growth of agriculture in the San Joaquin Valley and the discovery of oil in the area around Bakersfield. California's entire economy

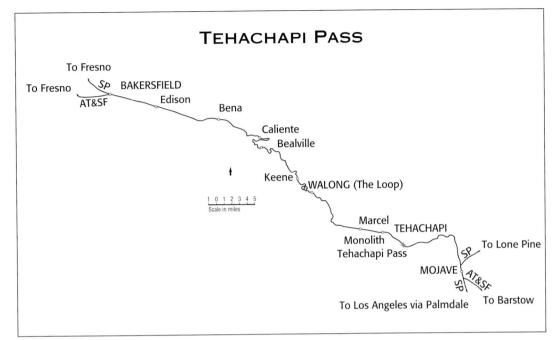

TEHACHAPI PASS

To Fresno
To Fresno
SP
AT&SF
BAKERSFIELD
Edison
Bena
Caliente
Bealville
Keene
WALONG (The Loop)
Marcel
Monolith
TEHACHAPI
Tehachapi Pass
MOJAVE
SP
AT&SF
SP
To Lone Pine
To Los Angeles via Palmdale
To Barstow

1 0 1 2 3 4 5
Scale in miles

was expanding, and the boom in southern California added lumber from the Northwest to the traffic mix. A large cement plant was established in 1907 at Monolith, a few miles east of Tehachapi, for the construction of the Los Angeles aqueduct.

Passenger traffic on the line was largely the province of Southern Pacific. In 1912 Santa Fe established a pair of overnight passenger trains, the *Saint* and the *Angel*, between Los Angeles and San Francisco in competition with SP's long-established *Owl*. The all-Santa Fe route between Los Angeles and Mojave via Barstow was more than twice as long as SP's and included Cajon Pass. Running time between Los Angeles and San Francisco was about 2 hours longer than SP's *Owl*. The *Saint* and the *Angel* lasted only until the end of 1918. In 1938 Santa Fe inaugurated the twice-daily streamlined Golden Gate service between Los Angeles and San Francisco, but since those services used buses between Los Angeles and Bakersfield, they had no effect on rail traffic over Tehachapi. Most Santa Fe passenger service over Tehachapi consisted of through cars to and from Chicago-Los Angeles trains — almost always secondary Chicago-Los Angeles trains, such as the *Grand Canyon* and the *Scout*. Not until the inauguration of the *San Francisco Chief* in 1954 was the Santa Fe a significant competitor in the Chicago-San Francisco market.

In the steam era Santa Fe motive power was primarily several classes of 2-10-2s for freight trains and helper service and 4-8-2s for passenger. Santa Fe tried several classes of articulateds on Tehachapi, but with no more success than it had experienced elsewhere. Diesels appeared in 1943, about the same time Centralized Traffic Control was installed between Bena (15 miles east of Bakersfield) and Tehachapi.

Nature

California weather tends to be immoderate, especially in mountain passes that connect different climatic zones. The town of Tehachapi boasts that it has four distinct seasons. Spring brings a carpet of wildflowers to the hills; fall brings the apple harvest — but summer brings searing heat and winter often brings heavy rain and sometimes snow, driven by the winds that constantly sweep through the pass. (In recent years the wind has become a resource: the hills between Tehachapi and Mojave are covered with wind-powered electric generators.)

The railroad follows watercourses on both slopes, and every few years heavy rainstorms wash away part of the line. One of the worst such storms was in September 1930. When the line was rebuilt a line change was made west of Caliente that resulted in helper grades. The eastward helper district was extended west to Bakersfield, and the helper base that had been established at Caliente in 1925 was abandoned. (A similar flood in 1983 closed the line for 10 days.)

California geology is unstable. A major earthquake hit the area on July 21, 1952, damaging 11 miles of line above Caliente and collapsing some of the tunnels and damaging all of them. Traffic was immediately diverted to the Coast Line, and construction crews went to work. One tunnel was abandoned, with track bypassing it on a new alignment; another was daylighted (converted from a tunnel to a cut); and a third was partially daylighted. The line was reopened August 15 with temporary track bypassing a fourth tunnel.

Proposals

Through the years there have been proposals to improve the line over the Tehachapis or bypass it altogether. Early in the 20th century SP considered electrifying the line but abandoned the idea (in the mid-1960s SP reconsidered the idea and ran computer simulations, but again dropped the idea). In 1910 a line with easier grades was surveyed. It would have looped into the canyon east of Caliente and detoured northeast of Mojave to reduce the grade to 1.5 percent. Santa Fe liked the idea as much as SP did, but both roads were short on money at the time. In the 1920s portions of the line were double-tracked, but costs of that for the worst part of the line — the tunnels above Caliente — were prohibitive.

In 1923 the Santa Fe proposed a direct line between Bakersfield and Los Angeles, using Grapevine Canyon and Tejon Pass and acquired some of the land necessary (that route was used years later for Interstate Highway 5). Santa Fe also considered two alternate routes east of Tehachapi: a line southeast to Cajon Pass (later used by SP's Colton-Palmdale Cutoff) and another a line from Tehachapi south to Saugus.

In the late 1940s there was a proposal for a 25-mile highway tunnel between the San Joaquin and San Fernando valleys, followed by a proposal for two tunnels 10 and 13 miles long with a short space between them across the San Andreas Fault. A 1950 refinement of the latter proposal included space in the tunnels for aqueducts, electric transmission lines, and railroads. However, the grades in those tunnels would have been no better than those on the existing line, and the SP and the Santa Fe were not interested.

Suggestions for further reading:

Tehachapi, by Steve Schmollinger, published in 1993 by Boston Mills Press, Erin, ON N0B 1T0, Canada (ISBN 1-55046-063-3)

Tehachapi, by John Signor, published in 1983 by Golden West Books, P. O. Box 80250, San Marino CA 91108-8250 (ISBN 0-87095-088-6)

An eastbound freight curls around the horseshoe curve at Caliente to begin the climb over the Tehachapis. A four-unit set of F7s leads in this February 1951 scene; 2-10-2 No. 3840, built by Baldwin in 1921, is pushing on the rear. Photos by Stan Kistler, February 16, 1951.

An eastward extra consisting of 16 deadheading Pullmans climbs around the curve at Caliente. Obscured by the smoke is a diesel helper. Photo by Stan Kistler, February 16, 1951.

The eastbound *Grand Canyon*, behind a three-unit set of F7s, ducks under the Highway 58 overpass about half a mile west of Woodford. Photo by William J. Pontin.

Steam locomotives use water at a prodigious rate, and ascending freight trains had to stop at least once during the climb to replenish their water supply. It was a time-consuming process and it required stopping and starting the train several times on the grade. Engine 3844, a Baldwin 2-10-2 of 1921, takes on water at Woodford. Photo by Reginald McGovern, August 1948.

The four F7s leading this eastbound freight are 77 feet higher than the rear of the train as they cross over Tunnel 9, viewed from the downhill end of the tunnel. Photo by Donald Sims.

Two Santa Fe freights, both powered by FTs, meet at Walong siding, just east of the tunnel that forms the crossing in Tehachapi Loop. Photo by Frank Clodfelter.

Five GP9s cross over their train in this June 1960 view from the uphill end of Tunnel 9. Photo by Stan Kistler, June 26, 1960.

Hidden behind 4-8-2 No. 3737 are two of Santa Fe's three Fairbanks-Morse Erie-built units. All are working hard to lift train 24, the *Grand Canyon*, through Marcel on the way to the summit on August 29, 1950. Photo by Stan Kistler, August 29, 1950.

Train 60, the San Francisco section of the *Grand Canyon*, works upgrade behind a trio of Alco PAs at Cable. In the siding is a Southern Pacific freight headed by a cab-forward. Photo by William D. Middleton, October 14, 1950.

Four F7s help a trio of Alco passenger units lift train 23, the San Francisco section of the *Grand Canyon*, through Tehachapi Pass, just about where the ascending grade out of Mojave eases somewhat. *Trains* Magazine photo by Wallace W. Abbey.

A three-unit set of FTs has the assistance of an older 2-10-2, No. 965, built by Baldwin in 1904, 2 miles west of Mojave. Photo by Frank Kirby, November 1945.

The caboose is sandwiched by a pair of 2-10-2 helpers on this westbound freight at Warren, 6 miles west of Mojave. Photo by H. L. Kelso.

While a Southern Pacific switcher adds a caboose to a westbound freight in February 1954, an eastbound Santa Fe freight rolls down into Mojave with brake-shoe smoke indicating that the dynamic brakes of the F7s needed help from air. Photo by Richard Steinheimer, February 1952.

A four-unit set of F7s is coupled to the point of train 23, the *Grand Canyon*, at Mojave. *Trains* Magazine photo by Wallace W. Abbey, April 1953.

During the station stop at Mojave the engineer of the eastbound *Grand Canyon* reads his orders. Photo by Richard Steinheimer, 1950.

Two General Electric Dash 8-40CWs wearing the revived red-and-silver Warbonnet livery and a rebuilt SD45 with westbound containers in tow meet an eastbound piggyback train at Cable, 3 miles west of the town of Tehachapi. Photo by Ted Benson, May 22, 1992.

THE PASSES AS THEY ARE TODAY

Raton Pass

The highway between Trinidad and Raton, Interstate 25, parallels the tracks and for most of the way is in sight of them, but there are few opportunities for photography. You can't — or shouldn't — stop on the highway except for emergencies. Most exits from the Interstate (and there aren't many) lead down to unpaved roads closed by gates and no-trespassing signs, then back up to the other side of the highway.

Two exits on the Colorado side can put you close to the tracks. Exit 6 leads to a bridge over the railroad that gives a good view of westbound trains, and an unpaved road runs south a short distance along the east side of the tracks. Exit 11 leads to the village of Starkville, where the road crosses the tracks at grade. The road continues west across the dam that creates Lake Trinidad to Colorado Route 12 and Jansen, where Santa Fe interchanges with Colorado & Wyoming. The northernmost Raton exit offers a good view of trains in both directions, again from an overpass.

The only passenger train on the route is Amtrak's *Southwest Chief*, which runs west in the mid-morning and east in the late afternoon. Freight traffic over Raton Pass varies considerably and depends on the amount of traffic moving on the route through Belen. If the southern route is congested, intermodal trains are routed through La Junta and over Raton Pass. Santa Fe is double-tracking the southern route.

Cajon Pass

The railroads are paralleled through the pass by Interstate 215 from San Bernardino to Devore and I-15 from Devore to a mile above the junction with State Highway 138, and also by fragments of old U. S. Highway 66, now a historic road. The Interstate offers few glimpses of the railroad; old 66 offers good views. Route 138 east of the Interstate leads directly to Summit.

For years all SP traffic between Oregon and northern California on the one hand and Texas and the East on the other had to move through Los Angeles, right through the congestion of the city and the confluence of several SP routes. In 1967 SP opened a cutoff from Palmdale, south of Mojave, southeast to the summit of the pass, then down the south slope just west of the Santa Fe track to Colton, where it joined SP's route east to Yuma, El Paso, and New Orleans.

Between May and September 1972 Santa Fe constructed 3 miles of new line at Summit, eliminating several sharp curves and lowering the elevation of the summit of the line 50 feet. At the same time the road installed centralized traffic control between Barstow and San Bernardino, with both tracks signaled for bidirectional traffic. Trains can operate in either direction on either track, depending on traffic. In addition, minor relocations have occurred through the years to ease curves or move the tracks away from flood-prone watercourses.

The railroads through the pass are busy. Landlord Santa Fe operates about twice as many trains as tenant Union Pacific; UP, about twice as many as neighbor Southern Pacific. Amtrak's Chicago-Salt Lake City-Los Angeles *Desert Wind* is scheduled over the pass by day — about noon westbound and early afternoon east (as this book goes to press, days of operation are Sunday, Wednesday, and Friday westbound and Monday, Wednesday, and Friday eastbound). The westbound *Southwest Chief* (Chicago-Albuquerque-Los Angeles) is due to arrive Los Angeles just after breakfast and therefore encounters daylight in Cajon Pass only during the longest days of early summer; the eastbound *Southwest Chief* departs Los Angeles midevening.

Tehachapi Mountains

State Highway 58 follows the railroad closely from Mojave to Tehachapi Pass, then is farther away but still within sight of it as far as Keene. Woodford-Tehachapi Road lies close to the railroad from Keene east to Marcel and affords access to the loop. Secondary roads are adjacent to the railroad from Bena to Bakersfield.

In recent years sidings have been extended to accommodate longer trains — in some cases sidings have been connected — and double track has been signaled for movement in both directions on either track.

The line is quite busy, even though it has had no scheduled passenger since Amtrak began operation on May 1, 1971. The two railroads run about equal numbers of trains. Most eastbound freight trains have either midtrain helpers or pushers on the rear. Midtrain helpers are usually cut out at the summit a mile east of the town of Tehachapi; pushers may cut off just west of the town. Helpers then drift back to Bakersfield without trains. Helpers on westbound trains often continue to Bakersfield to assist with braking.

INDEX OF PHOTOGRAPHS